Copyright © 2017 by Jennifer Duehring
Storyboards copyrighted 2017 by Kayla Olson and licensed to Jennifer Duehring

All rights reserved. That reservation includes the right to reproduce this in whole or in part, to store it in digital or other formats and/or to reproduce it in other forms and formats, including in pictures, photos or other ways of depicting any of the material in here. No part of this may be reproduced, distributed or made available in any form, nor may it be stored or made available in any type of data base or retrieval system except with written permission of the copyright owner.

Protecting the copyright is one way you can show your support while expressing gratitude that work which takes months to complete can still be offered so that others can get a copy.

I may have referred to a few items or phrases in this book that may be trademarked, copyright protected or otherwise protected. No disrespect is meant from the use of them. What's more, it is not intended to water down or dilute the owners' rights.

No illegal intent is made. In fact, just the opposite. So please honor them too.

DEDICATION

To Mom …

Who taught me the true meaning of unconditional love.

To all the Daughters …

Who have lived through the pain of losing their Mom and whose courage and strength to keep going has made all the difference.

INTRODUCTION

The Embrace of Gratitude: A way of healing past pain ... to hope ... to happy for Daughters who have lost their Mom

Ahhhh, embracing gratitude ...

Sounds soft ... and light ... and warm, doesn't it? Actually, it can be just that and so much more.

The Embrace of Gratitude is a practice which gives each of us an opportunity to write about the things in life we are grateful for. It can be as simple as being grateful for the feeling of the sun kissing your cheek or as deep as being grateful for someone who has carried you when you just couldn't take another step.

On the journey of surviving the loss of my Mom, there are several steps I have taken to move past the pain to a place of hope and happiness.

Gratitude is one of them.

Gratitude is one part of the toolkit needed to help us ... refocus the pain, stop the self-destructive patterns, embrace a new perspective, improve our relationships with others AND ourselves and lead to a new, happier way of living.

But please don't let it stop here.

My experience has been that committing to all the steps on the path can change your life ...

So let's turn the page, jump in and do this together!

Love,
Jenn

Mom
mobile

Remind Me

Message

Decline

Accept

If I could speak to my Mom just one more time, I would tell her I was grateful for these things about her:

The people in my life who have carried me when I couldn't are:

Despite moments of it being a really, really, dark time in my life, I found happiness in:

These are 3 things I like about myself (the more you say about you, the better).

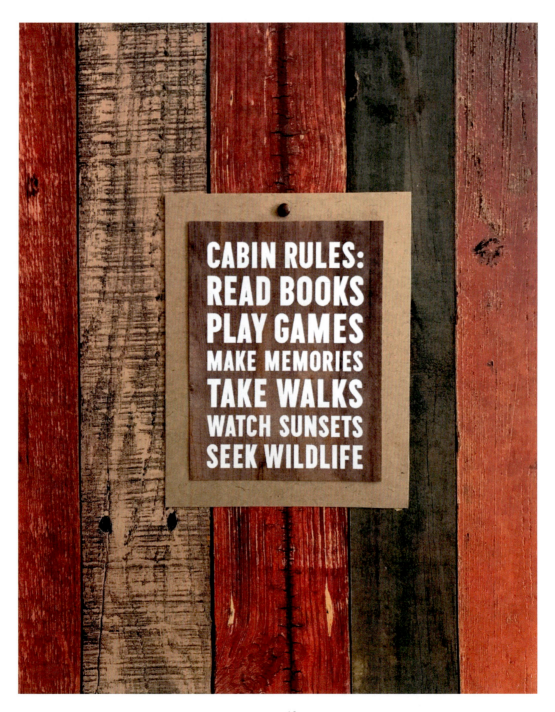

Write about three of your favorite family memories that involved Mom:

I am grateful for the following things that I attribute to Mom …
and here's why …

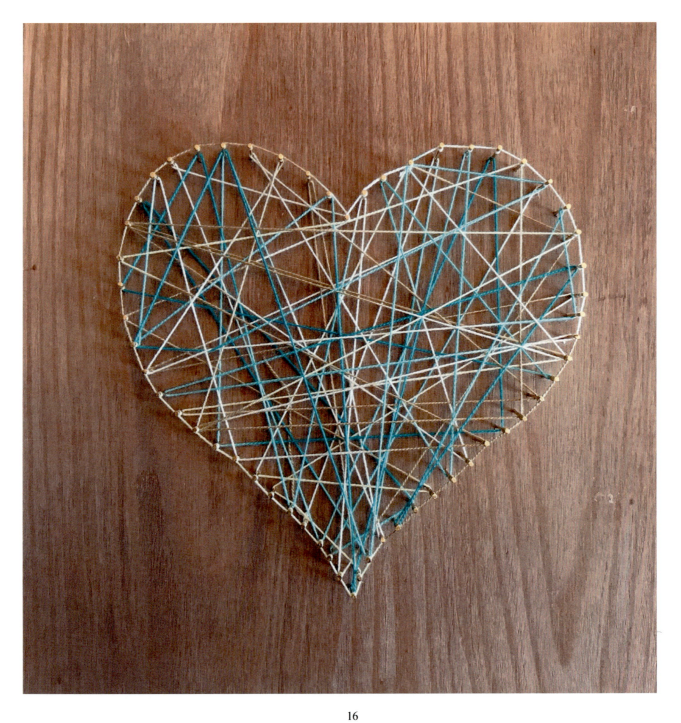

I am grateful for the ways my Mom showed me unconditional love by:

I felt happy when ....

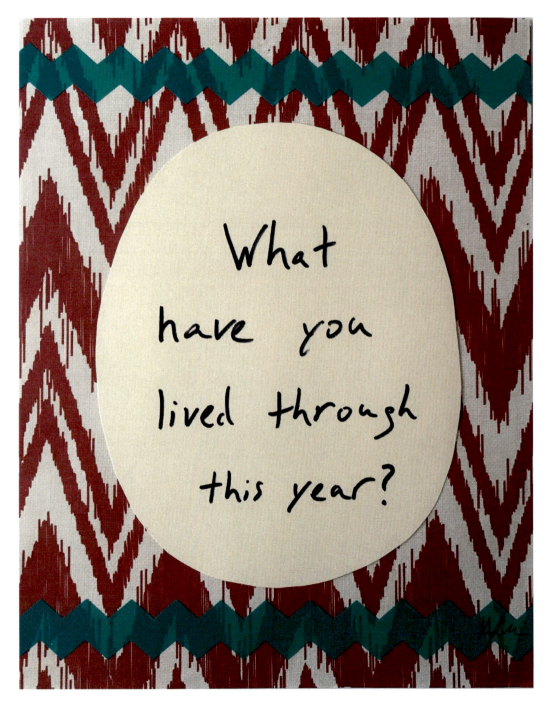

Some of the hard times I have lived through this year that helped form who I am are:

Some of the happiest moments I have lived through this year are:

Moments from this year that I would love to re-live over and over are:

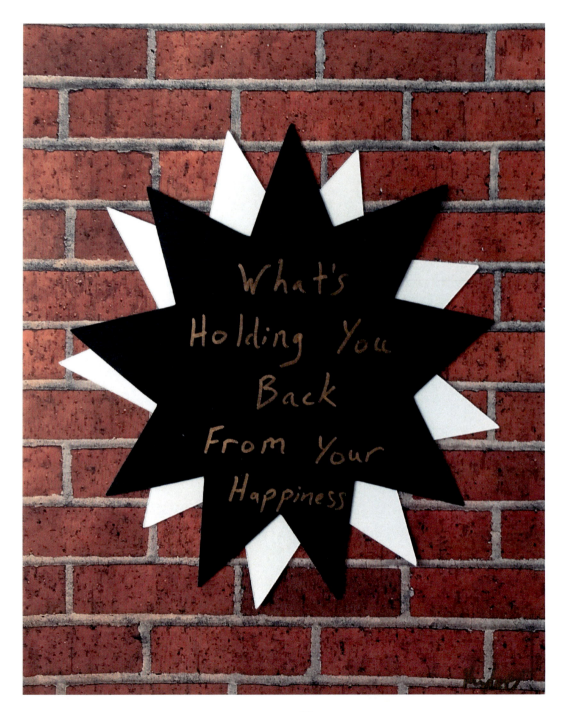

The top 3 things holding me back from my own happiness are…

Mom would not really have wanted me to be unhappy. So instead of going through life unhappy, I solemnly commit to myself, to Mom and the world, to take a step to do something about it.

Signed and committed to by _____.

Past pain ...

Thank you for coming this far in gratitude! I know some of the gratitude practice can be difficult and hard, as it forces us to comb through so much "stuff" about ourselves. Some of which has been buried for years. Yes, years.

Funny thing I have learned about grief is that no amount of numbing out to it keeps it from resurfacing. And by the time it does, we are a mere shell of what we were meant to be.

In my own story, numbing out for me meant taking care of and putting everyone else first, punishing my body through extreme diets and exercise that never worked and jumping into relationships where I gave up my own identity for that of someone else's. I had spent so many years numbing out to the grief, I couldn't even tell you three things I liked about myself when I began my own gratitude practice. That ... was a very sad day for me.

However, the good news about gratitude is, when practiced every day, it truly can change the way we feel and think about ourselves. For example, saying three things we like about ourselves each morning before we begin our day can completely change our mindset for the entire day.

I have read that in stable, balanced relationships, for every negative thought spoken it takes five positive thoughts to counteract the negative.[1] Crazy, right? But it's true.

So applying the same formula to the words we say to ourselves ... or take in from others ... is key. Because, after all, we do want to cultivate a stable, balanced relationship with ourselves, right?

Soooo, you have come so far ... let's turn the page and keep going ... together.

---

[1] John Gottman from The Gottman Institute is famous for providing the 5:1 ratio. www.gottman.com. Mr. Gottman found that for happy relationships, the ratio is 20:1.

The struggle ends when gratitude begins.

- Neale Donald Walsch

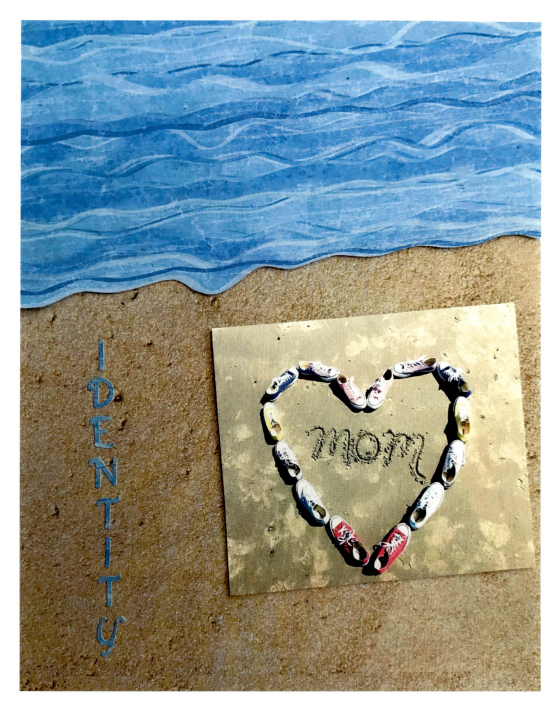

Each of us has our own very unique and beautiful identity that we let peek out in different ways. The parts of my identity my Mom would consider strengths are:

The parts of my identity I consider strengths are:

The identity I want to step into is:

Take What You Need

ENCOURAGEMENT | PERSPECTIVE | COMPANIONSHIP | FORGIVENESS | CREATIVITY | FRIENDSHIP | STRENGTH | HUMOR | LOVE | SUPPORT | PASSION | FREEDOM | COURAGE | PATIENCE | INSPIRATION | UNDERSTANDING | OPPORTUNITY

Sometimes being able to actually say what we need can be so difficult. It is made harder when we have an attachment to getting what we need from someone else.

Today I am committing to saying one thing that I need without regard to whether I get it, recognizing that practicing asking is more important in this moment than whether I get it.

That one thing is:

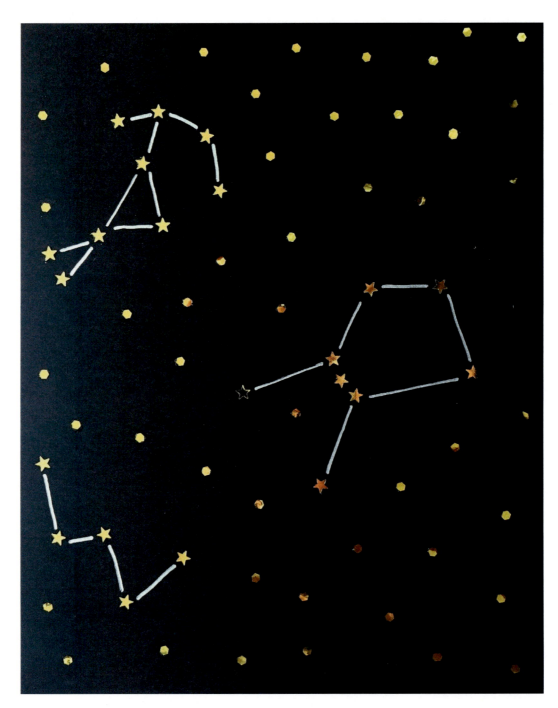

My Mom would wish the following for me:

To move to a place of gratitude, we may need to explore why we feel less than or what we are insecure about ... and especially how our loss of Mom influenced those insecurities.

If you could sit down with Mom right now and have her make everything alright, what insecurities do you have that you would share with her?

How have those insecurities shaped the person you are now for the better?

How have those insecurities held you back in the past from experiencing life the way you would like?

How do those insecurities affect the way you want to experience life in the future?

And …
How would you like to change your experience for the future
… to better honor you … and to better honor your Mom?

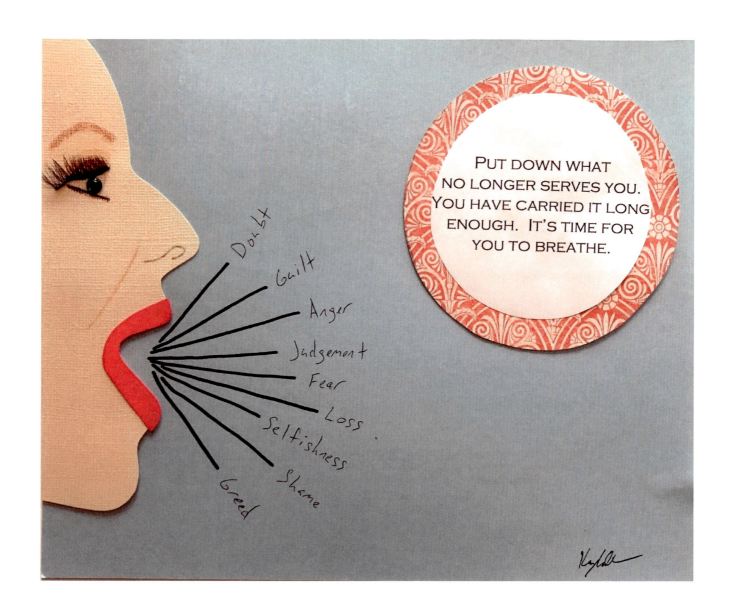

If Mom were here to hold you as you shared all of the heartache, pain and problems you have experienced, what would you share so that you could feel so much lighter?

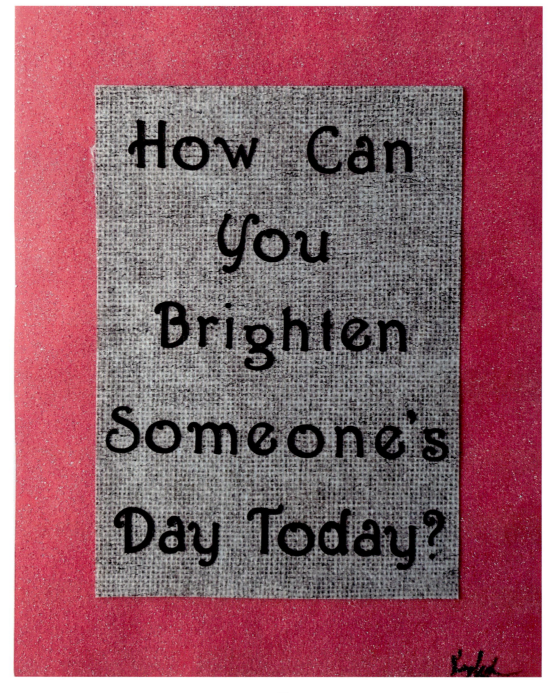

Start with someone else.

What are 5 things you can do ... that directly or indirectly remind you of Mom ... that can help make someone else's day brighter, more positive and just ... well, better?

Whenever I get down on myself ... or someone else does ... I can take in a deep breath, put my hand on my heart, and imagine Mom telling me I am so much more than good enough because:

I am inspired by the following friends, family, heroes, icons and world changers:

There are many things I received directly from Mom.

One is the way I show up when I am in touch with my emotions … when I access my full heart. Then, my heart stirs for people, places, experiences and dreams. Often times this appears as passion.

My heart has a passion for:

Sometimes we put ourselves, our dreams and our choices on hold as we mourn the loss of Mom ... experiencing life as though it comes to a complete standstill.

No matter how long or short the time we have been in mourning, we can simultaneously grieve and live our lives. Having a Bucket List can help us remember that.

A Bucket List is a list of things we want to do, see, or experience before the end of our own life.

My Bucket List starts with ...

To hope ...

Wow! You're already two thirds of the way there, can you believe it????

I can, and let me tell you why.

Gratitude has a way of taking us from being in constant pain to a place where hope actually lives.

In my own life, I have spent YEARS swirling in pain, and, in an effort to avoid feeling the pain, I numbed out with food, television, bad relationships, and the never-ending feeling that I had to save or fix everyone else. Sometimes (for a long time), I could completely escape it. Ultimately though, I ended up in the same bad relationship (just with a different person), repeating the same patterns, and found myself taking on someone else's identity once again. I had become defined by the pain and loss of my Mom.

I found that, through gratitude, I started to change. In combing through the memories of Mom, recognizing what she would wish for me in my life, and the power I have within me to stop numbing and start embracing ... my relationships started to change ... because I was seeing things differently.

Enter ... HOPE.

Our feelings and our memories are now front and center and we are starting to see the power we have within us to create a different path for ourselves.

Let's continue and embrace the final steps together.

Where flowers bloom, so does hope.

- **Lady Bird Johnson**

Some of my favorite memories of Mom are:

I honor these memories by:

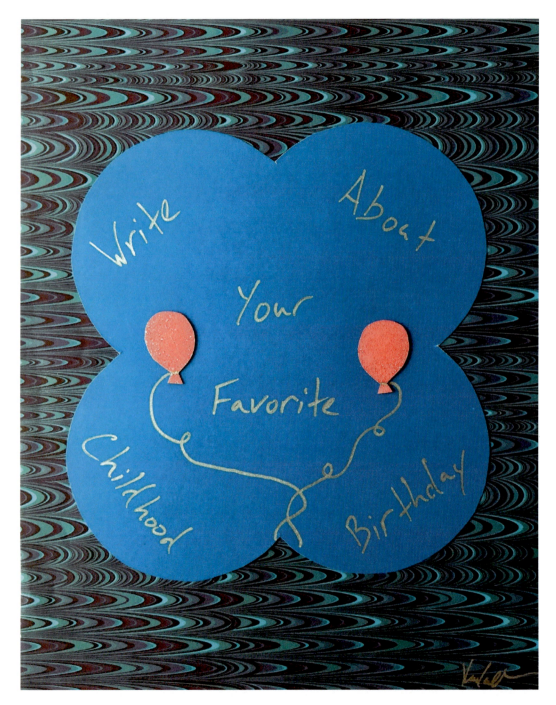

My favorite childhood birthday was:

And it was my favorite because I felt:

And that's because:

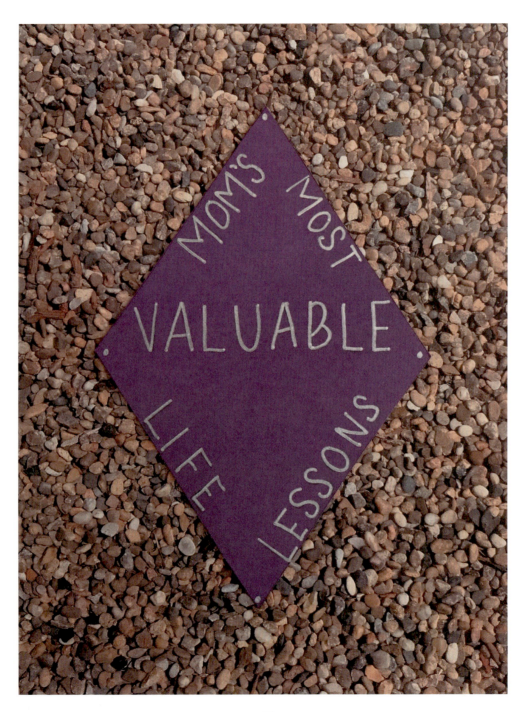

Mom taught me many things and the most valuable lessons I carry with me each day are:

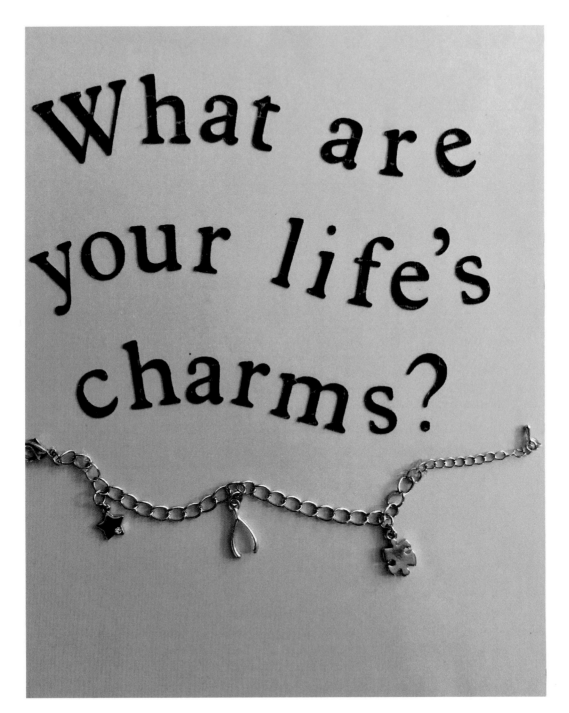

If I were creating my own charm bracelet, the charms that I would add are:

These are important to me because:

I am so grateful for the moments I have spent outside with my Mom doing:

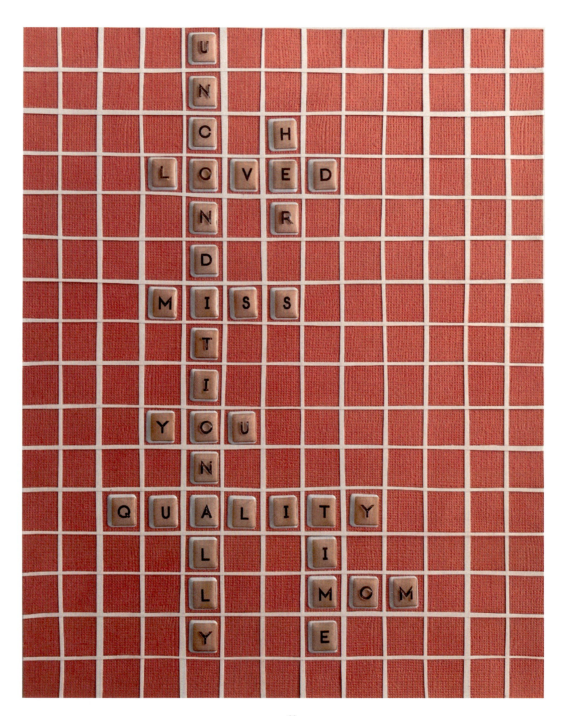

The activities I loved doing with my Mom are:

These mean so much to me because:

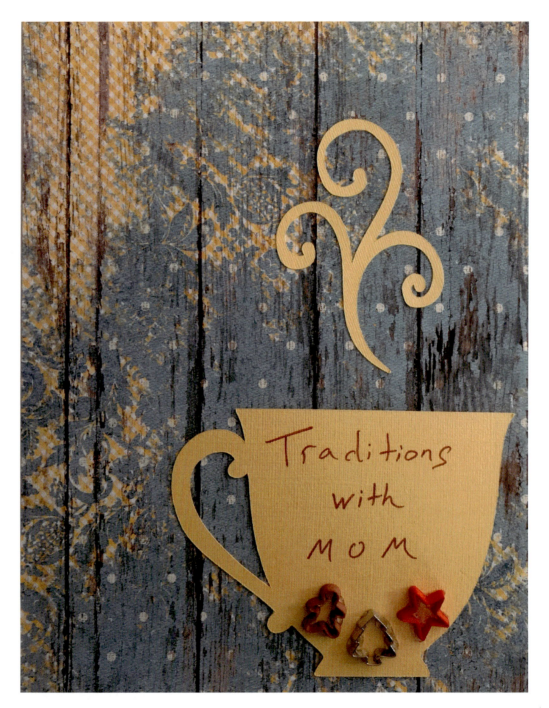

Write about some of your favorite traditions you shared with Mom:

I continue these traditions in my life today by:

I commit to honor myself and Mom by living each day fully and celebrating each day by:

Even though I may meet each season with excitement only to be counting the days when it is over, the changing seasons remind me that nothing is permanent and everything is to be cherished for its place in life's cycle.

I am so grateful for the following changes in my life:

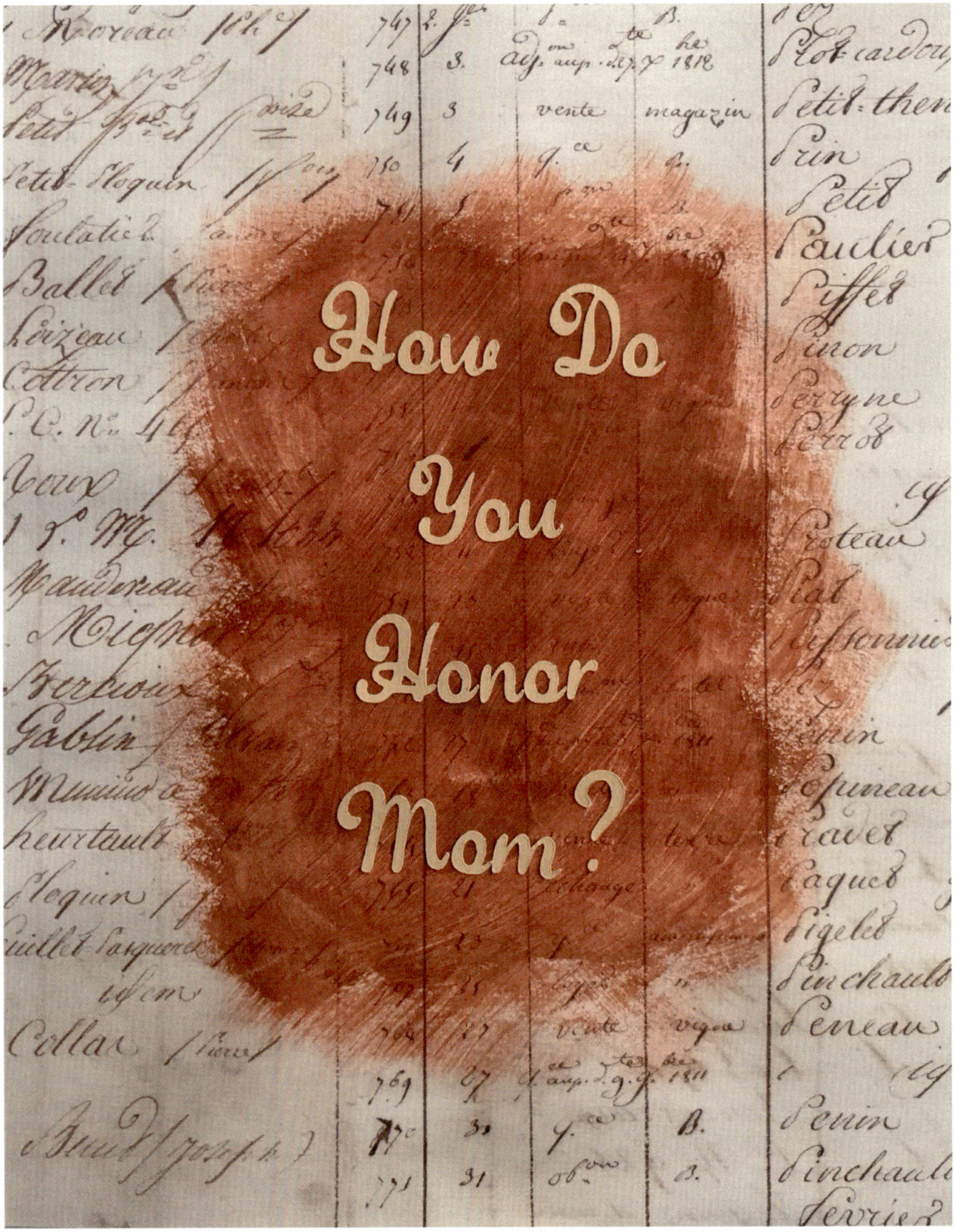
How Do
You
Honor
Mom?

Mom is not really gone. She is right here with me.

Some of the ways I celebrate the gifts she gave me, honor her and bring her presence into my life every single day are:

Wow! Where did the 30 days go?

If you and I were together right now - like at a coffee shop or at my home, we'd likely be talking about all kinds of things. Our conversation would touch on the pain of the past, the hope for our futures and how we were each experiencing our path towards joy. We'd share stories about our moms and how we are bringing more of her into our every day.

We might cry some. And we would laugh like crazy (you know, where the laughter goes so long and so hard that it winds up with one of us - likely me - letting out an embarrassing little snort and then can't stop. Yes, like that).

And then eventually we would get to the part of the conversation where we talk about what's next.

I am sure I would say something like 'Thank you for being on this journey with me and taking this important step toward hope to happy'.

We'd talk about continuing the momentum we got from the gratitude practice and we would commit to each other to keep doing it. But one or the other of us …. or maybe even both … would be worried that we were saying we would do it but wouldn't really. (Kind of like when I have said in the past I will lose weight or exercise but haven't really done it.)

And we might even talk about ways to bring more friends into it so that we really did this and so that gratitude became something of our journey that we shared with those we cared about.

We'd probably talk about how to go about doing that - the inviting our friends in part - and then it would occur to me that maybe we could do it together. And you would say something like 'How about we do it on Facebook so we could stay connected but we could do it at whatever time of day it worked for each of us'.

And I would be blown over by your suggestion because I really want to keep the gratitude practice going. And I know it is much harder to do it alone. So I'd jump at the chance to do it with you.

I'd be so excited that I would offer to start a private Facebook group so we could keep walking this walk together.

Hey wait! That's a great idea! Thanks for suggesting it.   Why don't I do that!?!?!?!

Please keep in touch on the private Facebook group I created to continue to support all of us on this journey. It can be found at:

https://www.facebook.com/groups/1498327956884428/.

In all seriousness, the journey past pain to hope to happy doesn't stop here. So please don't stop.

Join me. Don't just start and stop at the Facebook group, let's lock arms and do this together.

I would love it if you shared with me what other ways would help you on your journey.

Please reach out and drop me a note at embraceofgratitude@gmail.com.

Because you are worth it … and so much more.

Moving past pain … to hope … to happy.

Love,
Jenn

ACKNOWLEDGMENTS

To Mom ...

Who taught me how to hug ... you know, the kind of hug that draws you in, holds you close and makes you feel safe, warm and loved all at the same time.

Who taught me to appreciate the simple things in life ... like watching Singin' in the Rain together as a family and popping your own popcorn in a pot on the stove and baking Christmas cookies for an entire month and then giving most of them away.

Who made each day an adventure ... from the bike rides to the park on our way to tennis lessons to teaching us how to fish off the rocks by the ocean (not just the fishing part, but the whole deal of preparing the fish to cook) and to spending the afternoons at the beach followed by a dinner picnic on the sand.

Who taught me that nothing is too hard and how to roll up my sleeves and jump right in.

Who showed me the true meaning of unconditional love. I may have lost her too soon but I am so grateful for all that she was and all that she continues to be ... as she lives on in me.

To Dad ...

Who demonstrated how amazingly beautiful the gift of adoption can be.

Who taught me the value of learning and instilled a love of books ... by spending countless nights reading aloud when I was too young to do so and, in later years by taking me to the library and giving me the freedom to explore any subject I was interested in.

Who spent his free time driving my brother and me to our many activities, coaching my teams, cheering me on from the sidelines (even at 8am on a Saturday morning in a cold ice skating rink), to endless games of catch in the backyard, to playing Sorry for the millionth time, to exposing me to all different types of music (even the 'Bubble Gum' 80's kind) and teaching me about the stars and constellations from our own backyard.

Who put aside his own grief after Mom died and just kept going.

Who has stood by my side, given me a soft place to land, supported me through some really dark times and continues to cheer me on each and every day.

To Chris ...

Who may be the little brother, but has taught me so much more than I could've ever taught him, who always has my back, who provides thoughtful insight just when I need it the most, who knows how to make me laugh so hard that I just can't stop and has always been a confidant and true friend.

To Mom Sharyn ...

Who willing took on the Mom roll in my teenage and adult years, who bought me the prom dress I was so worried about buying when my Mom died and, in later years, who handmade my wedding gown, who demonstrates creativity, strength, courage and hard work in everything she does and who is not only my Mom but also a wonderful friend.

To Steve and Andrew ...

Who were never step brothers, but immediately my brothers and now amazing and supportive friends.

To Mom Jean ...

Who lives the true meaning of the word kindness ... whether it is in the form of a hand-picked bouquet of flowers 'just because' or the beautiful act of giving without the expectation of receiving.

To Mary ...

For your love and support on this journey.

On my own life journey, and in creating this book, I have been blessed with the help, inspiration, support, love and friendship of so many incredible people and, for this, I am profoundly grateful.

Alyssa and Aidan Pearson	Ann Marie Frasier
Norm Lamarre and Mike Downey	Marilyn Pride
Erin Pearson	Elijah Olson
Dawn, Pat and Brody Hannon	Nathan Olson
Shirley and Hugh Tyler	Gary Scott
Deb Cozzone	Edla Olson
Terry-Lynn Aplin	Jack Jones and Shawn Lundy
Kayla and Ben Olson	Barbara and Chuck Feldman
Joe Harrop	Margaret Robling
Carol DiCarlo and Paul Blanchette	Joe Napolitano
Kim, Jordan and Austin Barlow	Kim Ebner

Rich Medeiros

Stephen Flaherty

Deb Bettencourt

Susan Raymond Conroy

Gretchen Schwab Abrams

Kathleen, Bruce and CJ Brewer

Karen Altner

Rochelle, Nate, Nicole and Heather

Jeff Steele

Joel Levinson

Hope Edelman

Ray Edwards

Brené Brown

To Karin...

Who saw the spark from the beginning, helped me see it in myself, and has supported me every single day since.

To Kayla ...

Who not only designed each one of these beautiful gratitude boards, but has also been the inspiration for starting my own gratitude practice and who exemplifies the true meaning of gratitude in her own life ... each and every day.

Made in the USA
Middletown, DE
17 May 2017